INCREDIBLE INSECTS

BUGS

James E. Gerholdt

Published by Abdo & Daughters, 4940 Viking Drive, Suite 622, Edina, Minnesota 55435.

Copyright © 1996 by Abdo Consulting Group, Inc., Pentagon Tower, P.O. Box 36036, Minneapolis, Minnesota 55435 USA. International copyrights reserved in all countries. No part of this book may be reproduced in any form without written permission from the publisher.

Printed in the United States.

Cover Photo credit: Peter Arnold, Inc.
Interior Photo credits: James Gerholdt pages 5, 9, 10, 11, 13
                        Peter Arnold, Inc. pages 7, 15, 16, 17, 19, 21
Photo page 5 courtesy of Minnesota Zoo
Photo page 9 and 11 courtesy of Headwater Science center

Edited by Julie Berg

Library of Congress Cataloging-in-Publication Data

Gerholdt, James E., 1943
    Bugs / James E. Gerholdt.
    p. cm. — (Incredible insects)
Glossary and Index.
   ISBN 1-56239-480-0
1. Insects—Juvenile literature. [1. Insects.] I. Title. II . Series:
Gerholdt, James E., 1943- Incredible Insects.
QL467.2.G48 1995
595.7'52—dc20   95-1509
                                                              CIP
                                                              AC

Contents

BUGS

Bugs are one of the 28 insect orders. Insects are arthropods. Their skeleton is on the outside of their body. They also are ectothermic—they get their body temperature from the environment. More than 76,000 bug species are found worldwide.

Bugs are different from other insects because they have a beak. It is used for piercing and sucking food. All adult bugs have three body parts: the head, thorax, and abdomen. They also have six legs and two antennae.

Many bugs are plant pests and carry diseases. Others eat harmful insects.

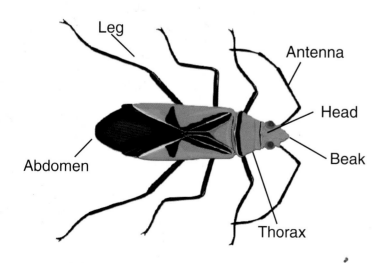

Leg

Antenna

Head

Beak

Abdomen

Thorax

Top Right: This white-eyed assassin bug comes from West Africa.

Bottom Right: Aphids are often found in gardens.

LIFE CYCLE

All bugs undergo a simple metamorphosis. This means that they hatch from an egg and spend the first part of their life as a nymph. They then crawl out of their skin as adults. Some species spend many years in the nymph stage, but most change quickly.

Almost all bugs hatch from eggs that are laid by the female. A few hatch inside the female and enter the world as tiny nymphs.

**Right:
A cluster of bug
eggs on a leaf.**

SIZES

Most bugs are tiny. Some are small. And some grow large enough to be scary! Leafhoppers and aphids are only 1/16 to 1/8 inches long (1.5 mm to 3.2 mm). But the lantern fly may be over 3 inches (7.6 cm) long.

The giant water bug is also large. It may be 2 inches (5 cm) long and 1 inch (2.5 cm) wide! They are often called "toe biters"! A cicada from Malaysia may have a wingspan of 8 inches (20 cm), but most are much smaller. A cicada from England is often less than 1/2 inch (12.7 mm) long.

Right:
The giant water bug can
become very large.

9

SHAPES

Bugs have many strange shapes. Some are long and slender, like the water striders and water stick insects. Some stinkbugs are almost round. Others have odd spines that look like thorns. The water boatmen have paddles on their legs that help them swim faster.

Right: The water scorpion is long and slender.

Left: Notice the paddles on the legs of this water boatman.

COLORS

Many bugs are colorful. Other species have shades that help them blend in with their surroundings. This is called camouflage. Even a bright green bug is hard to see on a green plant. Some bugs look like tree bark covered with lichen.

The most brightly colored bugs often taste bad, so they don't need camouflage. The bright colors are a warning to other animals not to eat them.

**Right:
This boxelder bug
has bright red eyes.**

13

WHERE THEY LIVE

Bugs live in many different habitats. Leafhoppers live on plants where they are hard to see. A cicada nymph lives underground until it is ready to metamorph into an adult.

Assassin bugs live in flowers, waiting for their prey. Froghopper nymphs live in foamy, spit-like nests in weeds or grass.

Giant water bugs live in ponds and other bodies of water. Water striders live on the water surface. Water boatmen live underwater. Every species has its own place in the world.

**Right:
Many bugs live
in flowers .**

SENSES

Bugs have the same five senses as humans. Their eyesight is good, and they can see things that people cannot.

Most bugs use their eyesight to find food and mates. Others use their sense of smell to find mates. Male cicadas sing to attract females. Leafhoppers also use sounds to find their mates. Many sense organs are found on the body surface, while others are located on the feet, mouth, and antennae.

**Right:
This May beetle
has very large
antennae.**

**Left:
Notice the
large eyes on
this bug.**

DEFENSE

Camouflage is an important defense for bugs. If the bugs look like their surroundings, an enemy can't see them.

Many have a foul taste and smell to keep enemies away. Other bug species bite their enemies.

Some, like the cicadas, can fly away from their enemies. Others, like the leafhoppers, jump to escape. The bugs that live in the water swim quickly to the bottom and hide.

Right:
This stag beetle's frightening appearance can scare away many predators.

FOOD

Bugs eat just about everything. Many are predators that eat other insects. Most bugs are ambush feeders, waiting on flowers and places that attract prey insects. Others, like bedbugs, suck blood from people or animals.

Plant-eating bugs are serious pests. Aphids can kill the plant on which they are feeding. Leafhoppers also feed on plants. They often carry diseases that can kill the plant.

Right:
A bug eating a leaf.

GLOSSARY

Abdomen (AB-do-men) -The rear body part of an arthropod.

Antennae (an-TEN-eye) - A pair of sense organs found on the head of an insect.

Arthropod (ARTH-row-pod) - An animal with its skeleton on the outside of its body.

Camouflage (CAM-o-flaj) - The ability to blend in with the surroundings.

Ectothermic (ek-toe-THERM-ik) - Regulating body temperature from an outside source.

Environment (en-VI-ron-ment) - Surroundings in which an animal lives.

Habitat (HAB-uh-tat) - An area in which an animal lives.

Insect (IN-sect) - An arthropod with three body parts and six legs.

Lichen (LIE-kin) - A plant that grows on rocks and trees.

Metamorphosis (met-a-MORF-oh-sis) - The change from an egg to an adult.

Nymph (NIMF) - The young of an insect that goes through a simple, or incomplete metamorphosis.

Order (OAR-der) - A grouping of animals.

Predator (PREAD-uh-tore) - An animal that eats other animals.

Species (SPEE-seas) - A kind or type.

INDEX

About the Author

Jim Gerholdt has been studying reptiles and amphibians for more than 40 years. He has presented lectures and displays throughout the state of Minnesota for nine years. He is a founding member of the Minnesota Herpetological Society and is active in conservation issues involving reptiles and amphibians in India, Aruba, and Minnesota.

Photo by Tim Judy